A 30-DAY DEVOTIONAL

8TH GRADE

LEADING THE WAY WITH THE "REAL YOU"

LARS ROOD

simply for students

8th Grade
Leading the Way With the "Real You"

© 2015 Lars Rood/0000 0001 2378 3544

group.com
simplyyouthministry.com

Credits
Author: Lars Rood
Executive Developer: Tim Gilmour
Chief Creative Officer: Joani Schultz
Editor: Rob Cunningham
Cover Art: Veronica Preston
Production: Joyce Douglas
Project Manager: Stephanie Krajec

ISBN: 978-1-4707-1824-4

11 10 9 8 7 6 5   23 22 21 20 19

Printed in the U.S.A.

CONTENTS

INTRODUCTION

This is it: the culmination of your middle school/junior high years. Finally you are at the top of the heap, the pinnacle at your school. It only lasts one year, and then you become a freshman. But there is so much you can do and accomplish in this one year. The goal of this 30-day devotional is to encourage you to lead well right now. You can do that by following Jesus more and leading yourself well. Then you will be ready to lead others.

I believe that you are at a place in your life where you absolutely can lead if you are given the chance. I want you to recognize that you matter, that your choices can make a difference, and that your contribution is huge. You can have an impact on this world right now. Don't believe that you have to wait until you get older. This devotional will include places for you to think deep about who you are and what makes you tick but will also push you to ask other people how they see you, what they believe most about you, and how you can receive other feedback from them.

HOW THIS BOOK WORKS

Each reading includes a short story for you to consider—something from my own life and experiences. I hope that hearing about some of my teenage struggles, wins, and life experiences will help you. Maybe you can learn from my mistakes, or at least feel like someone actually understands a bit of what you are going through. After each reading you'll find some follow-up questions to consider. You can do these by yourself, but you also can benefit from discussing them with a small group of teenagers, a couple of friends, a youth worker, or your parents. This book might become 30 weeks of curriculum or simply provide 30 days of focus before the school year starts.

Each devotion includes a section called "God Thoughts"—simple truths that come from the Bible and give you something to think about. Pulling out your Bible and reading it is a good, beneficial habit that will help you build a great foundation for your life. I'm convinced that you need to consistently hear that God is stoked about you and that God cares deeply about you as you own your faith this year.

You'll also find an action step called "Activate/Lead" in which I will encourage you to do something to discover and explore key truths. These ideas are focused on leading. Often they're ideas that take some effort to accomplish and can help you grow. I want to encourage you to really put effort into doing them. They'll help you draw closer to Jesus and discover what it means to lead others as you follow him.

It's my hope and prayer that these devotions challenge you, encourage you, and put you in places where you will have the opportunity to prepare for the future. If you are doing these with other people, I'm praying you have great conversations and opportunities to talk, ask questions, and kick around what it means to be a follower of Jesus.

SECTION 1

Following Jesus More Faithfully

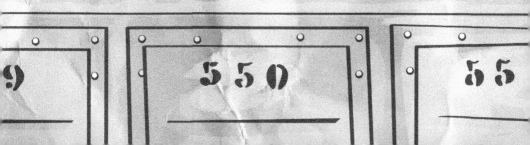

I sometimes get overwhelmed with faith stuff. I find myself looking at people who seem to have it more figured out than I do, and I wonder why. I wish I didn't get caught up in comparing myself with others—but I do. When that happens, though, I know what helps: Instead of trying to be like anyone else, I simply ask Jesus to help me be a version of myself that is more focused on him.

I don't know your faith story. You may be strong and focused and feel like you are in exactly the place God wants you right now. That's awesome, and I encourage you to stay focused. But maybe you feel like you are just missing something and want a stronger faith. Your eighth-grade year is a great time to make some focused steps in your journey of following Jesus. You have come through a year or two of middle school/junior high life and you have lots of that stuff all figured out. There aren't so many new things that happen in eighth grade, so it's a great time to focus on your faith and grow deeper as a Christ-follower.

What does it look like to follow Jesus more? It's kind of simple. Wherever you are right now, you can choose to go deeper. Just to be clear, though: When I'm encouraging you to take steps and go deeper, it's not because where you are right now isn't good enough. That's not the deal here. If you're already a follower of Jesus, that's a reason to celebrate—God loves where you are right now. My encouragement to follow Jesus *more* is simply to take a step in building a deeper, stronger relationship. It's similar to how it is with your friendships: There are always ways that you can grow closer to and build a deeper connection with your friends.

Eighth grade is a great time to focus a bit more on your faith because you have such a great opportunity this year to connect it to your life as the top grade in your school—and youth group, if your church has separate ministries for junior highers and high schoolers. Other younger students are looking up to you as they try to figure out how this faith journey works. You are a leader whether you recognize it or not. This is a great year to focus on this, too, because you will soon take that step to high school, where everything takes on a much greater seriousness—decisions you make will have an even more lasting impact on your life.

So here we go. Let's focus on some simple choices, habits, and steps that can help you follow Jesus more deeply.

WHY ARE YOU FOLLOWING JESUS?

I wasn't really sure how my faith and life worked together when I was in eighth grade. I'd heard a lot about how it was supposed to work, but on a practical, everyday level, I'm not sure if I had "experienced" what that meant. I was a fairly common youth group kid who knew a whole lot of Bible stories and had a pretty good foundation of faith. But I hadn't really been given many opportunities to live it out or to see how it could be real to my everyday life.

I wish I could say that eighth grade gave me a whole bunch of those experiences and I really understood it all, but that wasn't the case. No one pushed me to go beyond where I was to see if it would help me to grow to better understand what it meant to follow Jesus. I wish my friends and I had been given the opportunity to serve our church and community. I think that would have helped me understand what it meant to follow Jesus. I think it would have given me a practical understanding because I would have been doing the things Jesus told his followers to do. Jesus cares about hurting people. He cares about those who don't have food or places to live. I know now that following Jesus means I need to care about those things, too.

Following Jesus gives meaning and purpose to your faith and life. Growing deeper in that journey takes the "stories" you know and makes them more real. It allows you to think about the world from Jesus' perspective. It is why I tell eighth-graders that we want to give them "more" of Jesus because I want them to experience this and see why it will strengthen and deepen their faith.

Think About:

1. So, why *are* you following Jesus? Or if you aren't yet, what is holding you back from making that decision?

2. How has your understanding of what it means to follow Jesus changed in the past year or two? How might it still need to change?

3. What are two specific habits or actions that might help you to make your faith a bit more "real" in your life?

God Thoughts:

Read Matthew 14:25-32. In this passage we watch as Peter takes steps out of the comfortable boat to follow Jesus. What does this event tell you about your journey of following Jesus?

Activate/Lead:

Talk with a youth leader, parent, or other trusted adult about something you could do in the community to help people. Maybe you could serve at a food bank, shelter, or day care. Research it and plan an event where you and some friends can experience what it means to care for people.

HOW IS JESUS INVOLVED IN YOUR DAILY LIFE?

The adventure of following Jesus and seeing his presence in your daily life is helped by being focused and having some good patterns. I've seen some pretty amazing eighth-graders who've had this figured out pretty well—they truly have Jesus at the center of their lives. They have seen Jesus give them direction to understand how to love their friends, respect their parents, and care for the world. They share super practical examples of how their Christ-following friends encourage them to be solid examples and to have a good witness at their school. They text with friends and youth leaders and seem to really care about how their faith and life are connected, interwoven, and inseparable.

All of this plays out in how you lead, how you care about people, and how you set an example on the sports fields, in your classroom, in your extracurricular clubs, and in your neighborhood. It means you "live it" in your world—people can see that there is just something different about how you go about your life. It becomes more obvious because you are living for something other than yourself. When people look at you and wonder what you are all about, they just see Jesus living in you.

Think About:

1. What are three specific ways that your faith in Jesus impacts your daily life?

2. Is there anything you would like to add or change that might help you follow Jesus more deeply in your life?

3. Identify a couple of people that you know who seem to be doing this well—how are their lives impacting others?

God Thoughts:

Read Luke 9:23-27. What can you learn from this passage about how Jesus might want you to live your daily life as one of his followers?

Activate/Lead:

Think about one thing you could do at school tomorrow that would be a step for you in following Jesus more consistently and allowing him to impact each day. Write it on a notecard and then do it.

ARE YOU DRIVING, OR IS JESUS?

I've found this to be a great question to ask middle school and junior high students—*if you were in a car with Jesus, where would he be sitting?* This is one of those questions that can produce a ton of insightful thoughts and answers. I raise this question once with a small group of guys I was leading, and we ended up having some of our deepest and most insightful conversations.

Most of us spend a lot of time in cars. My first car was a green Volkswagen Bug. It was rusty, it didn't have a stereo, and the interior was mostly falling apart. But it was mine and I was pretty proud of it. I used to wash it and vacuum it out, which didn't really make much of a difference but felt good to do.

That car was similar to how my faith journey has been. It's not perfect. I've got some rust and tears, I'm not really flashy, and I don't have it all figured out. But I know that God has been with me the whole time and that God likes who I am and is proud of me just like I was of my car.

Now back to where Jesus would be sitting. (You thought I'd forgotten my point, didn't you?) Many times in my life I was definitely the one driving. I wanted full control of where I was going. But there have been other times when I have released control and moved into the passenger seat and allowed Jesus to take over. That ride just always seems to go better. And sometimes I've moved to the backseat, just allowed things to happen, and wasn't really concerned. That has led to other problems because I was disengaged.

I know you don't drive yet, but think through this analogy and how you can let Jesus truly be in charge. It'll help make your ride a whole lot smoother.

Think About:

1. Where is Jesus sitting in your car right now?

2. Where do you want him to be?

3. What's getting in the way?

God Thoughts:

Romans 8:14 tells us to be "led by the Spirit of God." That whole chapter (really, most of that New Testament book) gives insights on how to follow Jesus. Go sit in your family's car (seriously, go do it—though you may want to ask for permission first) and ask Jesus how you can let him to take the wheel and lead your life.

Activate/Lead:

At some point today, take an inventory of how much you believe Jesus has been leading your life and how much you've been the one taking charge. Write down three areas where you want Jesus to lead more than he is right now. Pray and focus on those areas. An additional challenge: Tell someone else what you are trying to do. This will give you an opportunity to lead others as you allow Jesus to lead you.

№.4

HOW CAN YOU LISTEN TO JESUS?

I've never been a good listener. Ask my mom, friends, teachers, and my wife. They will all tell you that I'm just not that good at it. A regular occurrence in our house: I'm getting ready to go to the grocery store and my wife and kids are telling me what to get, and then I forget what they said as soon as I walk out the door. I've learned that I either need to have them text me a list or I need to write it all out before I leave the house.

I'm a visual learner, which means I have to see it to learn it. This can make it tough for me to "listen" to Jesus. I get distracted when I'm trying to listen, which can make me frustrated and give up. Fortunately, I've learned some tips that have been helpful in this area. I know that for me to truly listen, I need to "look" so I can "hear" in places like the Bible. I will visually connect with what Jesus is trying to tell me by reading about him and asking God to teach me.

Let me tell you about a couple of specific ways that "looking" helps me to hear and recognize what God is revealing. First, when I read my Bible, I ask God to speak to me through it. Sometimes that happens when a particular passage or verse really seems to be right what I am dealing with at the time. Other times it's just a word or image from a Scripture that feels like God intends it just for me.

Second, because I am such a visually driven person, it often helps me to write or draw when I'm trying to listen. I'll either have my laptop open to a blank document or have an actual blank piece of paper in front of me, and then I'll just try to type or write or draw what I hear. It doesn't always make sense, but sometimes I get a stronger idea of what God is revealing.

I've also learned to listen through worship music because it draws me into a better focus. There are a whole bunch of other things you could do, such as going for a walk outdoors and asking Jesus to reveal things about him through nature and beauty. I don't think I've ever heard an audible voice from Jesus. Life sure would be easier if I had! But I'm still convinced that he speaks to me through reminding me of what I need to do, putting the right Bible passage in front of me, and through other people sharing truths with me.

Think About:

1. Have you ever felt like you heard Jesus? If so, what was that experience like?

2. If you haven't, in what ways have you tried to listen?

3. How could you remove some "noise" today as you seek to hear or understand or listen to Jesus?

God Thoughts:

In John 6:45 Jesus tells the people that if they "listen" to God the Father, then they will come to him. What Jesus is saying here is so important to us because it means that when we truly listen, God will reveal more about Jesus to us, and those truths will help us to understand better how to live a life that's centered on Christ.

Activate/Lead:

This idea may not be easy, but I think you will benefit from pushing yourself. Take a piece of blank paper and set it in front of you (or you can just use the space below). Now take five minutes and try to just listen. You might start out by simply praying, "Jesus, please show me what you want me to see." After those five minutes, write down what you saw, heard, or felt. Then share what you've written with a parent, friend, or trusted adult. Lead by sharing and being vulnerable.

WHAT LEADERS DO YOU ADMIRE?

I read a story once called *No Compromise*, about this musician named Keith Green. The book told all about his life as a Christian, and it really impacted me because it showed that you could be a follower of Jesus and experience success without having to compromise. I read this book at a time in my life when I was really trying to figure out my faith. Keith Green's story challenged me to be more aware of what kind of example I was setting.

Around the same time in my life, my youth group started going on more retreats. I loved to be around a couple of leaders who came with us on all those camps. They lived what I thought to be exciting lives: working during the week and hanging out with us eighth-graders on the weekends. Their faith was appealing, and they always seemed to be having fun. I wanted to live that kind of life, one of adventure and excitement. They showed me that faith didn't have to be boring.

Think About:

1. Identify three specific people whose faith you admire. Why do you admire them so much?

2. What characteristics do you find yourself most wishing that you had in your faith journey?

3. How can you find more people with great faith stories to learn from?

God Thoughts:

Hebrews 11:1–12:2 gives us an amazing list of faithful people from the Bible. Read through this Scripture and identify one or two specific things you can learn from them. To go even deeper, dig back into the Old Testament to read the full stories for one or two of those incredible people.

Activate/Lead:

Hebrews 12:1 tells us to "throw off everything that hinders." What things do you need to "throw off" because they're keeping you from growing in your faith? Take a piece of paper and write those things down on it. Then take that piece of paper and wad it up into a ball and literally throw it away. It may not fully get rid of those things in your life, but it is a great reminder of the decision you're making today.

WHAT DO YOU VALUE?

The other day I found my old coin collection in our garage, and I tried to give it to my eighth-grade son, Soren. He wasn't impressed. I told him it was something that I thought was really cool in middle school—and that some of the coins might have some value if he wanted to research them. My speech didn't convince him; he said he didn't really have any place to put them in his room.

I should admit a couple of things. First, the collection included an empty book for quarters. I had started collecting quarters but then decided that I would rather spend them on candy at school. Also, none of the other books for coins was complete. I really hadn't valued them all that much, and I didn't put a lot of work or effort into my collection. So when Soren wasn't really interested in the coins, I shouldn't have been hurt—because, honestly, they weren't truly valuable to me.

Value is a weird thing, and in middle school the things you value can change frequently. You might be totally into something one month and not care about it at all the next. And placing value on "things" never really works out because things break, become outdated, or lose their appeal. But what if we place value in a different way? How might your life change if you started valuing characteristics that you see in Jesus? What if you began to think about the things Jesus thinks and cares about—and those became your values?

Think About:

1. What is one specific thing that you value a lot right now? Why do you value it?

2. In your faith journey, what are some things you've been told to value?

3. Most of us are introduced to "values" by our parents or an older adult. How have these individuals influenced your own values?

God Thoughts:

Read 1 Timothy 4:6-8. This passage talks about where we need to place our value. After reading those verses, identify some of the Christ-like values that other people can see in you right now—and specific values you want Jesus to grow in your life.

Activate/Lead:

Go to your room! (Yeah, I just wanted to say it like that.) Then spend a couple of minutes looking around. Can you tell what things you value by what you have in your room? Now look around again and look through a lens of your faith journey. Is there anything in your room (or another spot in your house) that reveals how your faith is valuable to you? Maybe it's a picture from camp, a Bible you got when you were younger, or just a trinket or memento. Take a few moments to talk with God about why that thing has value to you.

WHY WOULD JESUS BELIEVE IN EIGHTH-GRADERS?

As I write these words, I am thinking a lot about the start of a new school year. And I realize that you be having a tough time figuring out how your faith and your school life will connect this year. I didn't have it all figured out at your age either. I was really struggling to make those things line up, too. I went to youth group and church every week, but somehow I didn't fully understand how I was supposed to be different at school. Honestly, it frustrated me sometimes because my faith was important but I just didn't know how to live it out in a visible, meaningful way.

But something happened to me in eighth grade that helped make things clearer. That year, I really felt Jesus was giving me a better understanding of who I was as a person. Until that point I'd always struggled to find my place and just "be myself." But suddenly I felt like my time at church and youth group surrounded by friends and youth leaders who knew me meant that I really had people speaking truth into my life.

I started to understand that God had given me specific gifts, talents, skills, and passions—and as I began to focus more on those things, I started to become more comfortable and confident. It really changed things for me. I more clearly understood that Jesus really thought eighth-graders were great and that we were capable of a whole lot more than we thought.

Think About:

1. How might following Jesus in the eighth grade look different from following him when you were younger?

2. Do you think you can make a difference that honors Jesus this year? If so, in what ways? If not, why not?

3. How could you tell someone that Jesus believes in him or her? Be as specific as possible.

God Thoughts:

Read Mark 1:16-18. I love this Scripture because Jesus is calling some young people to follow him. We don't know exactly how young these first disciples were, but I love thinking about how Jesus believed in these young people and recognized that they could have an impact in the world "fishing for people."

Activate/Lead:

I'm convinced Jesus believes in you as an eighth-grader. Just as he called young people to be some of his closest followers, he is calling you to have an active faith and to lead. What are three things you could do this week that would tell other people in your grade that Jesus believes in them, too?

WHAT INSPIRES YOU?

When you're 13 or 14 years old, inspiration comes from weird places and sometimes doesn't make much sense. When I was in eighth grade I somehow became convinced that my future career would involve computers. So that year I wrote letters to every computer/software manufacturer that I could find an address for and asked them if they would send me information on how to pursue that path. I received few replies, and most of those responses were just catalogs. I quickly decided that particular future was lame and chose to be a teacher instead—and later became a youth pastor.

I'll be honest: For better or for worse, I'm easily inspired. When I watch the Olympics or other sporting events, I find myself wanting to do what those athletes can do. When I read a biography about someone who's done something really cool, I get inspired to try new things, too. But my inspiration rarely makes it to the implementation stage. I learned that maybe I was being inspired by the wrong things.

Today I want you to think about your faith and what things inspire you to grow deeper and to more passionately follow Jesus. Maybe this is the first time you've thought about it that way. That's totally OK and a great place to start. Maybe you've thought about this before but need some encouragement to keep moving forward. That's OK, too, because all of us need to regularly think about what can inspire us to grow closer to Jesus.

Think About:

1. Identify one new thing you've been inspired to do in the last two years. What inspired you? How long did your new habit or hobby last—how did it turn out?

2. What places or settings seem to fuel your inspiration in your faith journey?

3. Who in your life inspires you? Why? How can you meaningfully share that with him or her?

God Thoughts:

Read 1 Thessalonians 1:1-3. In this passage Paul, Silas, and Timothy tell a group of Christ-followers how their faith, love, and endurance were inspired by hope in Jesus. I love how these guys are specific in their praise, calling out particular traits that were inspired by Jesus.

Activate/Lead:

Think about that passage from 1 Thessalonians 1 and how someone might call out traits in you that they see as "inspired" by Jesus. What things do you think they would identify—or what things do you want them to see in you? Find someone that you can talk to and ask that person what traits they see in you that are inspired by Jesus.

NO. 9
WOULD OTHERS FOLLOW YOU?

I wish I could talk about how my character, skills, concern, and strength caused people to want to follow me when I was in eighth grade. I wish I could share a story about how people flocked to follow me as I followed Jesus in an incredible way. But no—it wasn't like that. I didn't have a bunch of people who followed me. I know, however, that I was starting to figure things out as an eighth-grader.

The place where I began to learn to lead and felt like I was making a difference was in my youth group. We had a really small group of eighth-graders, and at the time only seventh-graders were with us in our youth group. One thing I offered that group was my consistency. I don't think I ever missed youth group or Sunday school. I was always there.

Because of that commitment, I started receiving some responsibilities for our activities and events—nothing major, but I knew that our adult leaders viewed me as someone they could trust to simply be there. So that was my start. I was consistent and that was the reason people began to follow me. I want to encourage you, too, to think about why people might follow you as an eighth-grader.

Think About:

1. What are some ways you have been a leader?

2. In what specific ways might you lead as an eighth-grader?

3. In your walk with Jesus, when have you felt like you were leading others toward a deeper commitment to him?

4. If you had the opportunity to lead anything, what it would it be and why?

God Thoughts:

Joshua 1:6-9 is one of my favorite passages in the Bible to comfort me and inspire me to lead. I love how God tells Joshua to lead—and the way God gives instructions about how to do that. Read that passage and see what it speaks to you.

Activate/Lead:

In that Scripture, Joshua is told to "keep this Book of the Law always on your lips" and to "meditate on it day and night." I challenge you today to memorize Joshua 1:9 and to write that verse in five places where you will see it every day. Read it, think about it, and believe that God will be with you "wherever you go."

NO. 10
WHAT CAN YOU LEARN FROM YOUR PARENTS AND OTHER ADULTS?

I once heard someone joke that after she graduated from college, her parents seemed to have gotten so much smarter. The joke, of course, was that as a teenager, she didn't think her parents had much figured out at all. But when she got older, she realized how wise her parents really were.

I can relate. When I was in eighth grade, the last people I wanted to get advice from were my parents. I'm pretty sure that I wasn't alone in this—my friends and I talked about how our parents didn't seem to understand us and totally didn't know what it was like to be a teenager.

I wish I could convince you right now that your parents are really wise and that you can learn a lot from them, but you probably don't really want to hear that from me. One thing I try to do with my own kids is to be honest about my failures, struggles, questions, and doubts. I'm not always perfect at doing this, but when I do it, I feel like our conversations go so much better. It's a better choice than acting like I have it all figured out, because that's when my kids listen to me the least.

But you're an eighth-grader and not a parent, so how can you make this work better? My advice is simple. Ask a lot of questions. Try to start dialogue and provide space for your parents or a trusted adult to give you some of their wisdom. It might not always apply and you may hear the same stories over and over again, but if you pay close enough attention, you'll discover wisdom, truth, and helpful ideas.

Think About:

1. What's one truly valuable thing that you have learned from your parents?

2. What things do your parents do that make you not want to listen to them? How might you talk with your parents about this?

3. What are two questions you want to ask your parents but you haven't because either you don't know how to ask or the questions would make you feel too uncomfortable?

God Thoughts:

Read Proverbs 1:8 and 4:1. These verses talk about the wisdom and teachings that we can receive from our fathers and mothers. Think about your own parents and what you can learn from them.

Activate/Lead:

Take a bold step today by talking to one of your parents or a relative and discussing something that you think they can teach you. Make a commitment to follow up with them and create space to learn.

SECTION 2

Leading Yourself

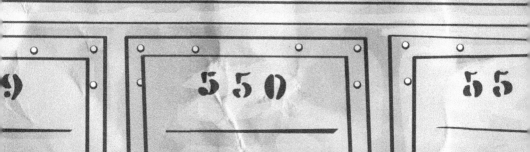

If you want to be the kind of leader who gives people a reason to follow you, first figure out how you can effectively lead yourself through your choices, actions, and lifestyle. Eighth grade is a great time to eagerly dig in and start figuring out what this looks like. Good patterns and healthy practices can be difficult to get started, especially if you are trying to create them at the last minute or when your life gets overwhelming. But so many of the patterns you establish now will have a huge impact on your high school experience and success.

In the first section of this book we talked a lot about the people you can be following and how to follow them. This next section will expand on that foundation by taking some of those ideas and connecting them more directly to you. We've already established that you need to focus on Jesus, place him at the center of your life, and allow him to guide your life. This section will help solidify those practices and guide you toward becoming the kind of person who will lead other people on that same journey.

Be warned: This may not be easy. My simple advice is to push through and see how these habits and actions can make a difference. Consider making a list of people and practices that could help you as you move into this section. If you need ideas on figuring it out, take the plunge and ask someone to help you. That's probably the biggest overarching theme in leadership that often gets lost—just because you are trying to lead doesn't mean you stop following others. Always look for help from other people!

HOW DO YOU MAKE CHOICES?

I still remember the day I had to choose. It was June, just before the end of seventh grade. I'd been thinking about it for a while, but was still trying to figure out the right decision. This was especially hard because I'd skipped the first year and felt like I'd be way behind everyone else.

What was the big decision? If I would play football in eighth grade. Football had never really been something that I was drawn to. But it felt different that year. I was going to be an eighth-grader, which provided a certain amount of freedom to try new things—and removed lots of my worry about what other people thought. Even though my last sports experience had been really tough—I had been cut from the seventh-grade basketball team—I really wanted to try this. But I struggled to decide.

Eventually, I took a piece of paper and made two columns. On one side I wrote all the positive things about playing football, and on the other side all the negative things. Creating the list took a lot of time, and the negative list ended up being twice as long as the positive side!

Once this list was done, I started praying through it. I don't really know if God cared if I played football or not, but I did think God cared about my list, which included things like "Being scared to fail," "Wanting to fit in," "Pleasing my dad," and "Believing I could actually be good at something." Those prayers ended up helping me work through who I was, what I valued, and where to turn when I didn't know how to make a decision.

Oh, and my choice? I played football as an eighth-grader.

Think About:

1. What tough choice have you made recently? How did you reach your decision?

2. When you think about your life, do you believe God has a set plan or path for you? Why or why not?

3. What are some places or people you could turn to when you're struggling with a big decision you have to make?

God Thoughts:

Proverbs 3:5-6 has been a major help to me over the years. This is especially true when I'm trying to figure things out and make important decisions. Read that Scripture and consider how it connects to you.

Activate/Lead:

While you still have your Bible open: If you have any kind of decision to make this week, grab a piece of paper and write out Proverbs 3:5-6 at the top. Then make two columns and identify the positive and negative things surrounding this decision. Next, pray through each one of these things. Then ask someone you trust to read through the list with you and offer some advice.

№ 12
DOES YOUR FAITH TRULY MATTER?

I really started to see people in my class begin to make bad decisions in eighth grade. Classmates started drinking, smoking, and making other unhealthy or unwise choices. I was given so many opportunities to try new things, and I didn't always do a great job of making the best choices. Fortunately, I had my faith to lean on, and my friendship with Jesus really made a difference in my life. He helped me and loved me even when my decisions didn't always honor him.

As an eighth-grader, I realized that my faith really did matter—my friendship with Jesus was important to every area of my life. When I was presented with choices and opportunities, I would think about my youth leaders, things I'd heard at youth group, and truths I'd read in the Bible, and I would pray for Jesus to give me help and wisdom. As I saw my faith make a difference in my life and be a solid foundation to build on, I felt so much more secure and stronger in who I was and what I believed.

I pray that you can experience that same kind of growth in your relationship with Jesus this year, as you discover how your faith can really matter in your life and at school.

Think About:

1. How much does your faith matter to your life right now? How do you know?

2. Give a specific example of how your friendship with Jesus has made a difference in your life.

3. What adult or friend is a good example of faith mattering in their life? In what ways do you see that?

4. How might a greater focus on "justice, mercy, and faithfulness" help your faith to matter more in your life?

God Thoughts:

In Matthew 23:23-24, Jesus condemns the Pharisees and other religious leaders, calling them hypocrites for focusing on the wrong priorities in life. He specifically says that what matters are "justice, mercy, and faithfulness." Read that Scripture and view Jesus' words in this passage as a starting point for considering how your faith matters to your life.

Activate/Lead:

Engage three people in conversation around this simple question: How do you know your faith matters in your life? It might be best to get them to answer in writing so you can reread their answers and think about how your life could or should model those same things.

NO.13
HOW CAN THE BIBLE HELP YOU LEAD?

Over the years I've owned many different Bibles. Why? Because I was always looking for the "right one" that would draw me in and help me focus on reading it more consistently and following its truths in my life. I've always wished that I had a Bible so worn out from use that it was being held together with duct tape. But that's just not the way things have worked for me.

I don't enjoy admitting this, but I really struggle in this area—not because I don't think the Bible is a great source of wisdom, strength, truth, hope, and leadership. I believe all of those things! I just struggle to set and keep a pattern of opening and reading it. When I am focused and reading regularly, it always helps me—I feel like that habit has given me exactly what I need.

As I read through the Gospels—the first four books of the New Testament—I'm particularly drawn to the places that talk about how Jesus retreated and spent time alone with God to recharge before and after teaching or performing miracles. This is one of the most important practices I have learned from the Bible that has helped me as a leader. Taking time to pray and talk with Jesus (and yes, open my Bible and read) sets me up to be better prepared to live it all out in my life.

Think About:

1. What passages, stories, people, or places in the Bible have been most significant to your faith journey?

2. How regularly do you read your Bible? How does this healthy habit draw you closer to Jesus?

3. In what ways do you think Jesus models leadership, and what can you learn from his actions, decisions, and words?

God Thoughts:

Read Mark 1:29-35. In this passage, Jesus performs many healings and miracles, and then the next morning he gets away to spend time with God. Consider what it might look like in your life to practice this habit, too.

Activate/Lead:

As I've said before, patterns can be hard to establish. But this week, make a commitment and choose a time that you can get away and be with Jesus each day. During this time, read your Bible, write in a journal, listen to music, or just walk and pray—whatever draws you closer to Jesus.

NO. 14
ARE YOU ASKING OTHERS FOR WISDOM AND ANSWERS?

Growing up, I often turned to my friend Evan's dad, Bill, for wisdom and answers. Bill was present in a lot of different areas of my life. He taught English at the junior high. He also led the choir at my church and was involved in my Boy Scout troop. On top of that I spent a lot of time at their house with Evan.

When I was in eighth grade, I really thought I had a lot of things pretty well figured out. I had bought into the lie that relying on myself was all I needed. This wasn't true, and that led me into risky and unwise situations a few times. Maybe you can relate.

Now, I didn't spend a lot of one-on-one time asking Bill questions and getting great, insightful answers that instantly changed my life. Instead, I simply watched how Bill led his life. I saw him interact with people, teach school, talk around a campfire, and work around the house. I learned a lot from him just by watching and observing. Bill lived his faith in a way that taught me how to be a follower of Jesus. And when I did have questions, Bill had helpful wisdom and answers.

I hope you have people in your life like Bill to watch and turn to when you need wisdom and answers. Don't try to do eighth grade alone.

Think About:

1. Who has helped you gain wisdom and find answers in your life? Give examples of how that person has helped you— or how multiple people have helped you.

2. When have you tried to figure out things on your own without asking for help? Give examples of how that has worked—or how it has created problems for you.

3. What steps can you take to find more people who can help you with wisdom and answers?

God Thoughts:

Read Deuteronomy 4:5-8. The author says people need to follow God's decrees and laws, and that these habits will produce wisdom. What does this Scripture tell you about how and where you can look for wisdom?

Activate/Lead:

How can you establish a regular pattern of asking friends, parents, or trusted adults for wisdom and advice? Who can you go to this week and ask to share wisdom and answers with you?

NO.15
HOW ARE YOU A LEADER ALREADY?

Chances are good that you are already a leader somewhere in your life—even if you don't realize it. These would be areas where you have some sort of influence, leadership, or high level of involvement. You will likely have even more opportunities to step into leadership during your eighth-grade year in clubs, sports, activities, youth group, or places where you work or volunteer.

My first significant leadership role came during my eighth-grade year when I was a patrol leader in my Boy Scout troop. No, that probably doesn't sound glamorous or cool, but for me this was a big deal. I led six other younger scouts at our meetings and also on campouts. I'm sure I wasn't the world's greatest leader, but that experience taught me a lot about how to lead.

I learned that leadership is hard. I have never been very patient, so my Boy Scout leadership experience was really tough sometimes. Trying to run a patrol meeting when everyone is running around and not wanting to listen—that wasn't much fun. I learned the importance of consistency with those guys and always tried to make sure that I was prepared and had some sort of plan.

As you think about leadership this week, focus on the things that you believe you do well and also the areas where you tend to struggle. I'm convinced that some of the best leaders are people who fully understand their struggles and failures, and then work hard to minimize those things.

Think About:

1. Where in your life do you currently lead in some kind of way?

2. How have you learned to lead? What people have helped you lead well?

3. This year, where would you like to step into a greater role of leadership? How can you make that happen?

God Thoughts:

Read Romans 12:3-8. This passage contains a lot of wisdom about gifts, skills, roles, and leadership. Rewrite this Scripture in a way that reflects your current responsibilities—and the God-given talents that help you lead well in those areas.

Activate/Lead:

To lead well, you need to understand yourself and know what your gifts and skills are. This activity has two parts. First, write out what you think your gifts and skills are as a leader. Second, ask someone who knows you well to write the same list about you. Compare those two lists, and discuss the results with the other person.

ᴺᴼ·16
ARE YOU TOO YOUNG TO LEAD?

As I've already mentioned, your eighth-grade year will bring many opportunities for you to lead. But some people your age believe their leadership skills are limited because they're too young—they have to be older to really make a difference. I want to encourage you that there is no reason why you can't use your gifts, talents, and skills right now to lead and do amazing things.

A few years ago I was introduced to an eighth-grade guy who was described to me as an abolitionist—someone passionately committed to ending modern-day slavery (yes, slavery still exists in our world). I was amazed at what he was able to do while he was so young. Leadership isn't always doing big things like that, though. It might be that you are simply called to lead in an area closer to home, or in ways that help your school or community. Regardless of how and where you serve, leadership is important because you can influence and help people and situations.

When I read through the Bible, I'm reminded of a core truth that Jesus talks about: We often are given leadership over small things first. After we learn to lead in those small areas, then we can be given bigger areas. It's a matter of earning trust and proving that we're reliable and faithful. This was true of the eighth-grade abolitionist that I met. He started small before he began to change the world. So where can you start?

Think About:

1. What leadership opportunities do you think you might be given this year?

2. If you were asked to dream really big about an area where you wanted to have influence or leadership, what would it be—and why?

3. How have you led so far in your life? What did you learn from those experiences?

God Thoughts:

In Matthew 25:14-30, Jesus tells a story about a master giving money to his servants and how the master responds when he finds out what they did with it. Read this Scripture, and then think about areas where you have led in small ways and how others have responded to you.

Activate/Lead:

Pick an area of your life where you have some leadership responsibilities. Spend a few minutes thinking through this area, and decide on three things you want to make sure you focus on as you lead—such as patience, kindness, or pre-planning. Write out your three and share with someone who is involved in that area with you, and ask that person to help keep you accountable.

NO.17
WHAT HAPPENS WHEN YOU CAN'T DECIDE?

You will experience some times in life when decisions just feel impossible. Maybe you have two equally great opportunities, and after writing out your lists of pros and cons, you just can't decide. You might even find that after you've prayed and talked with other people, you still don't know what to do.

This happened to me once when I was presented with two great summer opportunities and I just couldn't decide. All my anxieties and doubts came up—I didn't know what to do. At the time, I was frustrated with God because he wasn't making things clear. But later on I realized that God had simply given me a great gift of two incredible experiences and left it up to me to decide which one I wanted to do.

Sometimes that will happen to you, too, in eighth grade and in the years beyond, as you encounter so many different opportunities and choices. Here's my simple message that I hope will encourage you: Even if you're unsure which option is better, you can't lose. If you are following Jesus and it's clear he is in it, you win regardless of which thing you pick.

But you also might face times when you aren't choosing between two things. For example, maybe you have one specific opportunity but you don't know if you should take it. After all your process of figuring it out, ultimately you will just have to decide. That's part of the reason why it is so important to truly "know" yourself and have a good understanding of your gifts, talents, skills, hopes, and dreams. If you even understand a few of those things, that will help you decide.

One quick reminder, though: Sometimes we make wrong decisions. Guess what? Even when that happens, Jesus still loves you, and he promises to never abandon his followers.

Think About:

1. What recent decision have you struggled with and didn't know what to do? How did you eventually decide?

2. How well do you feel like you "know" yourself? What are three things you know are true about you?

3. Identify a time you believe you made the wrong decision—how did you recover from or work through that situation?

God Thoughts:

Sometimes when we are struggling with a decision, it is helpful to remember that we ourselves are chosen—that God loves us deeply. Read 1 Peter 2:9 and think about what that Scripture means for you.

Activate/Lead:

Chose an older person and ask about times he or she felt stuck and couldn't make a decision. Talk about how that person eventually worked through that situation. If you have a current experience you can share with this person, do so and see what he or she thinks.

№.18
WILL YOU EVER FULLY "GET IT"?

The simple answer to the above question is no. That's why we will always need Jesus in our lives. If we fully "got" everything, then we likely would become self-dependent, which can lead to a whole bunch of other problems such as pride, arrogance, and self-centeredness.

I wish that when I was in eighth grade, someone had simply told me that there would likely never be a point in life when I would have everything figured out. For some reason I was convinced that eventually I would reach that place in life—and that reaching it was a big part of what maturity and growing up were all about. I now know how much of a lie that was.

So here is just a quick reminder: You need Jesus to constantly be your truth, the center and focus of your life. When you waver from that, you will likely struggle. You just can't do it alone. Another way to look at this is to say that if you understand the truth that you will always need Jesus, then maybe you actually do "get it."

Think About:

1. What are three specific things you have learned about life that are really helping you?

2. What are two areas of life that you still haven't figured out well but you really need help in?

3. Who in your life models what it means to always rely on Jesus, and how have you seen them do that?

God Thoughts:

Read 2 Peter 3:18. This verse reminds us that we need to keep growing in our friendship with Jesus. This doesn't mean just when we are young. It means *always*. And remember that as you grow closer to Jesus and continue placing him at the center of your life, he will reveal more truth to you.

Activate/Lead:

Sometimes it is important to proclaim and call out truths in order for them to become more real to us. Today I want to encourage you to do that. What things do you believe to be true about Jesus? Find someone who is younger than you and tell him or her why you believe those things.

NO. 19
HOW DOES EVERYTHING ALL FIT TOGETHER?

I'm always intrigued by how God uses different things in my life to lead me toward his amazing plan for me. If you would have asked me as an eighth-grader if there would ever be a time when I would feel comfortable talking in front of huge groups of teenagers, I would have said no way. I also never thought I would ever write a book or even have anything to say that I felt was worth passing on to anyone. But God had and has a plan way bigger than I could imagine.

I got a taste of this during my middle school years through a few experiences. For example, I've already told you that I decided to play football my eighth-grade year. What I *didn't* mention was that I wasn't very good, and after my freshman year of high school I quit and never played again. But those couple of years of playing had a big impact on me and opened up a whole new social group to me at school. Suddenly more people accepted me—and more importantly, I learned that pushing myself to try new things was a really important thing for me to do.

Now, I'm not going to say that eighth-grade football directly led to the writing of this book, but it certainly led toward me learning more about myself. And it also helped me begin to see how God can fit together a bunch of seemingly random choices or events to ultimately lead us in the direction he wants us to go.

Think About:

1. What are some pieces of your life that are starting to fit together and make sense?

2. How well do you think your faith journey, school life, and other pieces of your life connect with each other?

3. Are there experiences or things in your life that you just don't know how God could ever use for good? Why or why not?

God Thoughts:

Go borrow a tool from the garage or your family's toolbox, and then hold it as you read Ephesians 2:8-10. This is one of those passages of Scripture that has always helped me understand how God is working in my life. If I am "God's handiwork" and he has "prepared in advance" the things he is going to have me do, then God must have a plan for how it all fits together.

Activate/Lead:

I think it's totally fine to ask God direct questions about what's going on in your life. Find a place where you can focus for about 10 minutes and ask God some very specific questions about what he is up to and how he is using things in your life for his purpose. Then spend about five minutes praying about what things God has "prepared in advance" for you to do and how you can see them.

№20
WHEN IS IT OK TO DOUBT?

Once again, I have a really simple answer: I think it's always OK to doubt. You may have heard a very different message your whole life. The church hasn't always done a good job of making teenagers feel comfortable when they have doubts.

Doubt is normal and common, and you shouldn't feel that there is something wrong with you if you experience it. As an eighth-grader you are experience so much in life. Your body is growing, your mind is expanding, and you have brand-new experiences and decisions thrown at you each day. You are in one of the most difficult but also exciting times of your life. It shouldn't be surprising that doubts emerge as you're facing all these changes and experiences. I'm a pastor and I've gone through times of doubt and wondered if things I've been taught are all really true.

One key piece of advice that I share with anyone experiencing major questions about faith: Don't go through it alone. Talk with people who have gone through that same journey, and discuss how they kept following Jesus. There also might be times when what you need to do is just be comforted by other people's strong faith, and allow that to be enough for you during that time.

Think About:

1. What area of faith causes you to have the most doubt— and why?

2. Do you think people in your life are OK if you express doubts and struggles with your faith? Why or why not?

3. How might you be able to get answers or help when you are struggling with doubts about the Bible, God, or what it means to follow Jesus?

God Thoughts:

Read Luke 24:36-39—a passage that talks about Jesus showing up to his disciples after his resurrection and helping them with their doubts. If the people who were the closest to Jesus and knew him well still had doubts, then you can be confident that it's OK for you to have times of doubt, too.

Activate/Lead:

If you attend a youth group or Sunday school class, talk to your leader about holding a "Doubt Event." You can be creative and lead this time in a bunch of different ways. The goal is to provide space for other teenagers to express their doubts and not have anyone step in and try to answer all their questions. Instead, each person can simply share his or her doubts, talk with others experiencing the same thing, and pray that God will reveal answers and truth to them in his time.

SECTION 3

Leading others

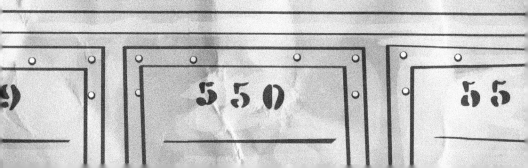

By this point in our devotional, you've probably realized that leadership isn't easy. I've been leading for a long time in a bunch of different settings, and I still find myself in situations where I just don't feel like I led very well.

When we lead others, we are given a big responsibility. Other people may scrutinize your every move. They will watch to see if what you say as a leader lines up with how you live your life. I have always been convinced that the students in my youth group learn more about what my faith is like when someone cuts me off in traffic than by what I teach during youth group! Leadership is revealed and defined by how we respond to real-life situations.

You can do it. With God's help you can do amazing things. This can be a really exciting season of your life. Many of your experiences have led to this point where you can begin stepping into greater positions of responsibility and leadership. Use your place and position in the right way and see what can happen.

NO. 21
LEADING YOUNGER PEOPLE

This is probably the most common type of leadership opportunity you will have as an eighth-grader—maybe on a sports team, or a school club, or a youth group activity, or somewhere else. This can be the easiest type of leadership to get comfortable with, but it also comes with a couple of major added pieces that you will have to navigate. Understanding who you are and how your faith in Jesus impacts your life is huge here because that's a big piece that people will be watching.

I totally failed in this area when I was in eighth grade. I was given responsibility over an activity at youth group and had to share what was important to me as a follower of Jesus. As I shared, the younger brother of one of my friends was listening, and I sensed that he knew I wasn't being totally truthful. He had watched me live, talk, and interact with others for years so he totally knew that what I was saying wasn't accurate or authentic.

Another piece you have to be aware of is that younger students will sometimes follow your lead without thinking about whether you're making wise or unwise choices as a leader. Be aware of your actions, words, and decisions because they can have a big influence over younger teenagers.

Think About:

1. Identify a time you did something in front of a younger person that was inconsistent with what you believe as a follower Jesus. If you could do it over again, what would you do differently?

2. What does it look like to model Jesus and your faith journey in all areas of leadership?

3. If you have been given any responsibility leading younger people, give examples of what you have done and what the experience was like.

God Thoughts:

Romans 12:9-13 talks about a bunch of different traits and habits that are important for followers of Jesus. Read that Scripture and then consider which two things in those verses might be most important as you lead younger people.

Activate/Lead:

Leadership is less about *what you do* and more about *who you are*—at the end of the day, your character and beliefs are what people will remember most. Grab your phone and type a note (or send yourself a text) with five characteristics that you want to be known for when you lead. Look at that note regularly, and anytime you are given a chance to leader, review your list and pray about it.

LEADING OLDER PEOPLE

The last time I ever went skiing with my grandfather, he was 91 years old. I was so terrified that he would fall and get hurt. I tried to encourage him to take it easy and go down an easy slope. But he wanted to go straight to the black diamond run—the hardest run we could choose. Even though I thought it wasn't a good idea, I went with him—and we had a really good time. He didn't fall on the run—but I did!

I learned from that situation that when I lead older people, I really have to spend time getting to know them and their skills before I pass judgment or make decisions about what I think they can or can't do. Leading older people can be tough because they will often have more wisdom, skills, history, and abilities than you do.

Fortunately, we have examples of Jesus shaking up the belief that young people can't or shouldn't lead people who are older than them. Jesus chose young disciples and gave them authority, power, and responsibility over many older people. Jesus was less concerned with status or cultural norms than with devotion and belief. So when you are in a situation where you have to or get to lead someone older than you, remember that you can learn from them as you lead—and remember that God has given you gifts, talents, and skills to do this.

Think About:

1. If you were suddenly given leadership responsibilities over a bunch of people older than you, would you feel comfortable or uncomfortable? Why?

2. What specific gifts and talents do you have that could help you lead people who are older than you are?

3. How can you both learn from someone older than you *and* lead that person at the same time?

God Thoughts:

Read 1 Peter 5:5-9. This Scripture tells us about how we need to "submit" to those who are older but also practice humility "under God's mighty hand." Jesus calls us to be leaders who honor others and also look to God for strength and help.

Activate/Lead:

Wise leaders often create some sort of advisory board or group of people who can provide wisdom and support when they need it. Identify two people that you could ask to be on your "board" who can help you understand how God wants you to lead. How can you then invite them into this journey with you?

NO. 23
LEADING WITH YOUR GIFTS

Some people are just good at lists. They're the organized ones who always seem to have all the details figured out and plans set so that things just go right.

I am not one of those people.

But I am good at making sure that we have adventures along the way. This has generally been true during my years as a youth pastor. I know that my gifts line up more with having vision and passion for something, but I'm not really good at the planning and implementation of my ideas. That's why I recruit people to help me handle those kinds of details— people who are skilled, talented, and gifted at it.

When you lead, it's important to know what your gifts are. Put yourself in leadership situations where those gifts are useful and valued. Because if your gifts don't line up with how you are being asked to lead, you will frustrate yourself and those you are leading.

Think About:

1. What are three of your God-given gifts and talents that can apply to leadership?

2. How have you experienced God using your gifts and talents in a positive way?

3. Have you ever been asked to lead in a way that just didn't line up with who God made you to be? How did you handle the situation?

God Thoughts:

Read 1 Peter 4:10-11. All followers of Jesus have received gifts. Figuring out how to best use those gifts to serve and lead is a key part of growing up. How would you summarize the main message of those two verses?

Activate/Lead:

Think about your gifts, skills, and talents. Ask a couple of people where they could see you leading successfully, and why. Take time this week to pray that God would give you meaningful ways to lead as an eighth-grader.

№24
LEADING WHILE STILL FOLLOWING

Never stop following.

That's probably one of the most important leadership ideas you can learn. You may reach a place later in life where you feel like you have things figured out. It's really important that you resist the temptation to put yourself at the center and stop looking to Jesus for direction. The times when I have believed that it was "all about me" were the times I have struggled the most.

And this isn't just something that happens with teenagers. Recently I began to have breakfast once a week with someone older than me. During these times, I share things that are going on in my life and ask him for insight and wisdom. It's been a really valuable addition to my life because he has provided me with a Jesus-focused perspective in some areas that I just couldn't see. These kinds of conversations can benefit you, too.

Think About:

1. Who or what do you follow that really helps you stay focused on your faith journey and helps you grow closer to Jesus? Why?

2. As you transition into eighth grade, how easily might you lose focus on Jesus and try to do things on your own?

3. What steps do you need to take to make sure that you are still "following" while you are leading?

God Thoughts:

Matthew 14:25-31 tells about a time Jesus walked on water and Peter stepped out to go to him. Read that Scripture and think about what Peter did that caused him to begin to sink. How might Peter's experience connect to us as leaders?

Activate/Lead:

Find someone older than you and invite that person to breakfast or coffee. Ask him or her to help you think through something in your life. Invite this person to share Jesus-focused wisdom with you. This might be easy to do, or it might be a tough step. You can ask a parent, coach, relative, teacher, youth pastor, church member, or anyone else who is following Jesus.

№ 25
LEADING AFTER A
"WRONG" DECISION

I remember it like it was yesterday.

I was with a group of friends at the county fair. It was the last day, and vendors were trying to sell off all their remaining food and drinks. My friends and I were sitting on a bench about 20 feet from a booth where someone was selling drinks. They shouted, "Ice-cold lemonade, ice-cold Cokes" over and over again. My friends and I were trying to talk but couldn't hear each other because of the vendor. I thought she might quiet down a bit if I bought a drink. So I bought one, but she kept shouting.

As I sat with my friends, I grew more and more frustrated hearing her yell, and all of a sudden I threw a piece of ice that somehow—from 20 feet away—hit the vendor right between the eyes. This was a bad decision. I was shocked and didn't know what to do—so I ran away. That was another bad decision. I actually went home and hid because I was so ashamed at what I had done.

You probably have a similar story of something that went wrong and impacted you in a negative way. It's really important to remember that God is about forgiveness and second chances, and these bad decisions don't have to define who we are.

Think About:

1. What effect did a specific bad decision have on you? How would you handle things differently today?

2. When you think about leading and making decisions, how does being responsible for others make you feel?

3. When you blow it and make a bad decision, how do you stay connected to Jesus?

God Thoughts:

Read Matthew 26:33-35, 69-75. Think about how Peter failed and how he must have felt. But Jesus also told him that he would be the "rock" that the church was built upon, and the book of Acts tells us how Peter became a key leader among the earliest Christians. How does Peter's experience encourage you?

Activate/Lead:

Figuring out how to lead despite a failure is an important skill. And it's not something you should have to do alone. Ask two people this week about ways they have failed and what God taught them through those failures.

NO. 26
LEADING AFTER A "RIGHT" DECISION

Most people can quickly remember a story about a time they made a "bad" decision. Those are easy because we tend to remember when things go wrong. It also can be easier to talk about our failures than to tell people about times we've been successful.

But I want you to take a few moments and think about a decision that you just know you got right. I often point back to the decision I made in eighth grade to consistently attend youth group and Sunday school. At the time, it didn't feel like a huge decision for me. It's not like I had a lot of other things happening on Wednesday nights or Sunday mornings. But it still was a decision that I made, and it's had significant, lasting results.

Because of that decision, my faith in Jesus is strong. I taught myself that going to church and youth group was part of who I was—not just an activity that I might do some weeks and not do other weeks. You could even say that this was a leadership decision because I was leading myself.

I wonder what good decisions you will make this year and how they will impact your life...

Think About:

1. What is one leadership decision you've made that you just know was right? How do you know that?

2. How much do you believe you rely on Jesus when you make decisions? Use a scale of 1-10, with 1 being very little and 10 being a lot.

3. Do you tend to think more about your bad decisions or your good ones? Why?

God Thoughts:

Read Psalm 25. What does this Scripture reveal about what we need to do in order to know what is right?

Activate/Lead:

Chances are good that for much of your life, other people have made decisions for you. But you will find out that as you get older, you have to make more and more of those decisions for yourself. Think about some practical, ordinary decisions you have to make this week. How can you make good decisions without having someone else tell you what to do? This is a great opportunity to have a discussion with a parent or trusted adult about your plan.

NO.27
LEADING WHEN YOU DON'T HAVE A CLUE

I've often been in positions of having to make decisions when I wasn't entirely sure what to do. Sometimes they've been silly things without huge consequences—such as, the elevator door opens and someone has to decide if we're going to go right or left. I figure that I have a 50 percent chance of making the right decision, so I'll just pick a direction and start moving.

But other times, the decisions have been more significant, and the simple method of just randomly picking one doesn't feel safe. You'll probably have to make some big decisions in life when you really just don't know what to do. At those moments, you'll be really glad to have a strong faith in Jesus and his leading in your life.

I believe strongly that as I focus on Jesus and allow him to lead in all areas of my life, my decisions don't feel overwhelming even when they are tough. When I have a really big view of God—believing that he is all-powerful, all-knowing, and in charge of absolutely everything—my decisions don't seem like such a big deal.

And the opposite has been true, too. When my view of God is that he is small, only exists in my church, and doesn't really impact my life, then my decisions seem so hard. Fortunately, in this faith journey you can choose how you view God. And I hope and pray that you will choose the really big view of God.

Think About:

1. What is one recent decision that you had a tough time making? How did you eventually work through it?

2. Think about a time you made a decision but then went back and started second-guessing your choice. Why did you do that?

3. Do you generally find it easy or hard to make decisions? Why?

God Thoughts:

Read John 8:31-32. How do you think following Jesus can "set you free"?

Activate/Lead:

Start a new habit today: Every time you have to make a decision, ask Jesus what you should do. Yes, I mean *every* time. Do it in the simple, mundane things as well as the hard, significant things. If you don't hear or sense a response, the next question you can ask is "How does Jesus' teaching impact this decision?" You might find that this changes your perspective on what to do when you don't have a clue.

NO. 28
MAKING UNPOPULAR CHOICES

As you get older and take on leadership roles, you'll likely find times when you just can't please everyone—you'll have to make some unpopular decisions. But *knowing* this doesn't really help you feel good about it when it does happen!

I can think of a couple of unpopular choices I had to make while in middle school. The first was pretty simple and just involved being honest with my parents about where I was and what I was doing. I was with a couple of friends who didn't want any of our parents to know what we were doing. We weren't even doing anything wrong; they just wanted to be free from their parents and not tell them everything. But my parents had given me only a couple of rules in life, and I knew that if I broke them that there would be big consequences. So even though my friends didn't want me to, I told my parents what was going on.

Another unpopular choice—a more serious one—happened a couple of years later when the party scene became a bigger deal in my hometown. I didn't want to be around it very much, so I made the decision that I wouldn't go to many parties. This frustrated some of my friends, but I believed that following Jesus and going to a bunch of parties just didn't line up very well, so I stuck with my decision.

As you serve and lead, you will find yourself sometimes having to do what is right even when it's not what everyone wants. The key is figuring out how to make these choices and explain your reasons in ways that people will understand, even if they don't like it.

Think About:

1. When have you made a choice that wasn't popular with others? Why wasn't it popular—and why did you make it anyway?

2. When you've had to make unpopular choices, where did you find encouragement and support? If you haven't faced this yet, where might you find encouragement and support?

3. What unpopular choices have others made that have affected you? How did you respond to them when they made those decisions?

4. Have you had to make any decisions because of your faith that your friends have not been happy about? If so, what did you learn from that experience?

God Thoughts:

Mark 10:17-23 tells us about a young man who really wanted to follow Jesus but wasn't prepared to make the kind of sacrifice Jesus wanted. This young man chose to walk away and not follow. Read that Scripture, and then consider what sacrifices Jesus might be asking you to make as you follow him.

Activate/Lead:

When you read the Gospels and follow Jesus' journey, you see that he often made choices that angered people. Think and pray about any tough choices you have to make right now in your life and how your faith in Jesus can help you. Write out three ways that your faith can influence you to make right choices and encourage you, even when those decisions are unpopular.

NO. 29
FOLLOWING JESUS IN A NEW DIRECTION

As you go about your eighth-grade year, you'll encounter new opportunities and things you could try out. You might like change and new opportunities because that's how you are wired. Or maybe you're not very good at moving in new directions and would prefer that things just stay the same all the time. Regardless, the key part of today's thought is *following Jesus* into something new.

I can't count the number of times I've moved in a new direction on my own that didn't really make any sense. This was particularly true the one year in high school when I decided to become a wrestler. I'm not sure why I thought this was a good idea—I was 6'1 tall and weighed about 145 pounds. I was a horrible wrestler and lost pretty much every match.

But I can point to other times when I knew Jesus was leading me and it was such a ride to be following him. In fact, this is how I ended up where I am at today. As I began to follow Jesus more with my life, he opened up some doors for me to use some of my gifts and talents that I didn't even know I had, in ways that he clearly had set up for me.

I wonder what new things Jesus might be asking you to follow him into this year and how your faith will grow because of it!

Think About:

1. Is there any new direction that you feel Jesus is calling you toward right now?

2. Have you ever gone in certain directions that were your own idea and not from Jesus? How did those turn out?

3. What are some ways that you can figure out if a new direction presented to you is really somewhere Jesus wants you to go?

4. How do you "put on the new self" as a follower of Jesus while still keeping the pieces of your life that you really like and value?

God Thoughts:

Ephesians 4:20-24 tells us we are to "to put on the new self." Read that Scripture and pray about how Jesus might be telling you that there are "new pieces" of you that he wants to show you this year.

Activate/Lead:

It's easy to get stuck in a rut. Change is never easy, even when it's something good. Find someone who knows you well and ask that person to help you come up with a simple plan that will help you move in the direction Jesus seems to be calling you this year.

PREPARING TO START ALL OVER AGAIN

The idea behind this final devotion might sound sort of depressing. Next year you will return to the bottom of the pack, as you go from being an eighth-grader to being a high school freshman.

But maybe look at it this way: You're actually being given an amazing chance as an eighth-grader to try out a bunch of things. And you have a certain amount of freedom this year to see what you like, what your gifts and talents are, and how you might still need to grow as a leader.

No matter what, you will be leaving a legacy after your eighth-grade year. What if you simply committed to following Jesus in any direction he wants to lead you? What if you looked for ways to learn a whole bunch about your faith, who you should be following, and a bit about leadership? Wouldn't that be a successful eighth grade? What kind of legacy would that leave for younger grades?

And you don't have to think that you are at "the bottom" next year. There are so many amazing things you can do as a freshman that can simply build off the ways you have grown and learned this year.

Take advantage of this eighth-grade year. Learn to try all you can. Next year will be different, so focus on just this one year.

Think About:

1. What are two habits you can pursue that will help you draw closer to Jesus and let your faith grow deeper this year?

2. How might God use the devotions in this book to challenge you to think differently about what it means to be a leader?

3. Where do you think you need help as a leader? What is a next step that can help you grow in that area?

God Thoughts:

Read 1 Timothy 4:12. How would you summarize and explain the big idea of this verse to one of your friends?

Activate/Lead:

How can you "set an example" for other teenagers through your speech, life, love, faith, and purity? Look for specific ways to take your answers and put them into practice this year.

CONCLUSION

You just made it through 30 devotions all about preparing you for eighth grade. As you went through the questions, Scripture, and activities, I hope that you learned a whole lot about yourself, your faith in Jesus, and your gifts and talents.

Obviously, this is just a starting block and not a map to explain everything. This short book was aimed at making you think but not thinking for you. You need more people and tools in your life to help you figure this all out. My advice is to find people who love Jesus and have walked a longer journey with him than you, and ask them a lot of questions. When you doubt and don't know what to do, lean on their wisdom and belief and trust in Jesus. You will find that as you do that, you'll begin to recognize more when you need to turn to others for help.

As I write these final words, I'm praying that you have an amazing eighth grade. There are so many opportunities in front of you. I love thinking about how you will be impacted and how you will impact others. I believe, without any doubt, that God can and will use you this year.

Never forget that you can have an impact as an eighth-grader. Follow Jesus and allow him to direct your path—and just see what happens.